Prairies of Possibilities

to Jeff & Jill,

Thanks,

Duane L. Herrmann

Other titles by Duane L. Herrmann

Ninety Years in Kansas

Whispers Shouting Glory

Early Poems

Andrew Herrmann Family in America
    (in German: Andreas Herrmann Famalia in Amerika)

Voices From a Borrowed Garden (ed.)

Fasting, the Moon and its Suns: a Bahá'í Handbook (ed.)

Statements on Writing (ed.)

The Life of May Brown, in Her Own Words

The Bahá'í Faith in Kansas, Since 1897

Fragrances of Grace

Early Bahá'ís of Enterprise

A History of the Bahá'í Community of Samarkand
    (with Dr. Hasan T. Shodiev)

A Family at the Turn of a Century

Ninety-five Years in Topeka, the Bahá'í Faith: 1906-2001

Kansas Vistas

'Abdu'l-Bahá Writes to Kansas City

Topeka Friends Meeting: 1982-2002

Selected Trees

A Little History of Islam in Topeka
    (with Imam Omar Hazim)

Book Three

Prairies of Possibilities

New and Selected Poems

Duane L. Herrmann

iUniverse, Inc.
New York Lincoln Shanghai

Prairies of Possibilities
New and Selected Poems

iUniverse books may be ordered through booksellers or by contacting:

iUniverse
2021 Pine Lake Road, Suite 100
Lincoln, NE 68512
www.iuniverse.com
1-800-Authors (1-800-288-4677)

Credits:

Some of the poems, or earlier versions, included in this volume were originally published in the following volumes or periodicals: *American Poets of the 1990s*, "BAFA, #25," *Creative Circle*, "East and West Literary Quarterly," *Fragrances of Grace, Hidden Roots, How to Use Potpourri in the Classroom*, "Inscape of Washburn University," *Just As the Wind, Kansas Vistas*, "Onomatopoeia," "Phoenix Sound," "Potpourri," *Selected Trees*, "Sunflower Petals," *Voices from a Borrowed Garden, Word of Mouth, Whispers Shouting Glory*, "World Order."

ISBN-13: 978-0-595-35051-3 (pbk)
ISBN-13: 978-0-595-79757-8 (ebk)
ISBN-10: 0-595-35051-8 (pbk)
ISBN-10: 0-595-79757-1 (ebk)

Printed in the United States of America

Dedicated to my mother without whom I would not have tried so hard.

Contents

FAMILY PLOWING

I plow the paper with a pen
engaged as the family has been
in cultivation: sowing and reaping.

I plow the paper with a pen,
in a solitary field—
it always has been.

My father was a farmer,
his father, and his before him;
we are plowmen in our rows.

I plow the paper with a pen—
rows of words across the space
in neat and even lines.

Though plowing is the family business,
my "machineries" now differ
for a different kind of crop.

But the plowing is the same:
long straight lines
across unmarked fields.

SPRING LAKE

Sitting on the rocks
    on the edge of the lake,
the water gently claps
    into holes and spaces.

The breeze bringing waves
    brings ancient sounds
that have survived
    the post-columbian age:

Thumping, thumping, rhythmic thumping
    drums and chants:
in clear and ringing tones
    through the opposite trees.

The chants of America:
    native words in native voices,
five hundred years endured,
    proudly raised once more.

In the clear evening sky
    the night queen sails,
smiles on children of the moon,
    knowing they will shine once more.

SPRING TOWERS

Towers of the Spring,
    rising billowy brown
    climbing high in the sky...

Hundreds of feet in the air.
    One here, and another there,
    another further on...

Altering the landscape,
    dwarfing trees and hills,
    on the scale of clouds.

On the plains
    they can be seen for miles,
    unique and awesome.

Tomorrow they are gone,
    vanished in the air;
    blackened earth remains,

Evidence
    of regeneration
    by prairie burning.

HOUSE ON THE EDGE OF A MEADOW

There is a house,
    a tiny house,
sitting on the edge of a meadow.

A round silver egg:
    it is the scene of visions.

Tender young trees
    nestle it softly
so the breeze will not die.

Trips here,
    to read, write and pray,
    lead away to vast spaces.

My Heart Sings.

To have a tiny house
    is to be real
        for a tiny time,
in the woods
    on the edge of a meadow;

The sky is huge!

AWESOME

On top of the prairie
  with the world all around
spread below:
  rolling hills and valleys,
lines of trees along the creeks—
  open spaces everywhere.
The sky is immense!!
  more bluer than blue.
The wind is forever
  caressing the grasses.
The spaces proclaim
  the vastness of God,
what other else
  could be so huge?
Life on the plains
  teaches humility and fragility
for it is clear
  that creation is so vast.

KANSAS NACHTLIED, GOETHE

There is a stillness
    over the hills and fields;
meadows lie baking
      in the heat.

There is no breath.

Birds are silent and the weeds
    grow lank and seed.

Wait!

The heat will feel you too.

SUMMER WETTING

The heat had been forever:
   constant oven-wind
      shriveled leaves and trees.

Cemented soil cracked
   in canyons reaching deep
      into the tortured earth.

No rain for more than weeks;
   moisture only dimly
      a faint and fragrant memory.

Suddenly from far away
   echoed muffled rumblings,
      and low dark clouds.

Salvation seemed too true
   to suspend parched lips
      or slack dry skin.

Eyes watched with hope and wonder
   as clouds relieved the sky
      from the searing sun.

A miraculous wall of wet
   advanced across the fields
      and, suddenly, was here.

God was good again.
   Steady showering filled
      pores and cracks and leaves.

The crops and life and animals
   were saved. The family
      would survive another year.

PRAIRIE HAWK

Over the fields and prairie,
    creeks and tree lines—
endless miles
    of countryside,
I survey my domain,
    All MINE! All MINE!
The wind past my eyes
    lifts me up or down.
A sound carries
    on the wind
and I know
    food is near.
I see motion
    and swoop down,
the meal…
    will be mine.

AH!
    Life is good!

WITNESS

The abandon building
    gray
weathered wood and warped
    still
erect, upright and proud
    here
on the side of the ridge,
    now
prairie all around—lonely,
    once
the seat of culture-learning
    pride
to become "Americans"
    this
was their school and center
    when
they knew who they were
    becoming.

GRANDFATHER'S ROAD

Invisible to the traveler now,
    two tracks through the grass,
but the discerning eye
    can see two fence rows on each side.

Across the prairie and down
    the hill it leads
over a little cement bridge,
    with iron rails;

One missing.
    Also missing is the house
and barn and windmill.
    Not even a line of stones.

His early life,
    his boyhood home,
has returned to the prairie
    from whence it came.

The earth
    reclaimed it's own.

But the road remains
    to show the way
to the past of my grandfather's life:
    he walked this way to school.

MAKING HAY

Mornings when the dew had dried
    Granpa mowed the prairie meadow
    going round and round and round,
        outside to center.

Early after lunch the boy would rake
    the now dry hay
    once around for Granpa's twice,
        outside to center.

Fluffed up windrows snaked along
    from sheets of new cut grass
    raking opposite the cutting,
        outside to center.

Once done, the hay was raked again
    merging two windrows to one,
    drying all sides of the grass,
        outside to center.

Father ran the bailer, especially—
    if the knotter had a temper,
    following the windrow
        outside to center

WAGON TALE

Driving down the rocky road
    something soon "feels" different
then a crashing in the bushes.
    Backward glance saw horror:

Brand new-built hay wagon,
    shiny, clean and perfect,
just finished days ago;
    now awkward in the ditch.

Heart with dread the boy confessed
    the accident on reaching home.
The father, solemn, listens
    with simply nodding head.

He seems to take loss well,
    thought the son,
all thumbs when working
    farm tools and equipment.

At the scene they start to clear
    brush to free the wagon.
"This has grown up some," says the Dad,
    "since I last lost a wagon here."

ON THE HORIZON

The tree on the rise of the prairie
    stands tall,
etched against the sky—
    it is seen for miles,
a solitary witness
    to life continuing.
This tree sees raindrops
    and the wind
as companions
    with the stars and grass.
The tree says:
    "I'm alive, I'm here, I'm now."
For "now"
    is the only time that is.
Now is the time we each have,
    the only time
to make our life
    and save our souls.

THE FAMILY HOUSE

I sought refuge
    in the family house:
walls of stone and love.

Windows rattle
    by blasts of wind,
but I was safe within.

I grew up
    but never away
from the house and farm.

Caring hands
    and listening eyes
welcome me back home.

MAGIC EVENING

The grandmother engineered the evening
without her children knowing:
"Yes, bring the grandkids over."
(four)
"No, I'm not going anywhere."
(one)
"Would you like to leave the children?"
(four more)
"That will be fine."
She smiled.

She did not hint to any
that she would be watching
the other's children.

One by one the cars stopped by
unloading children two by two.
When the last exclaimed,
"You should have told me…"
She replied:
"Go on, have a good time,
we'll be fine."

And we *were* fine:

All the cousins in one room
paired by age or interest
(the oldest read a book);
nothing for Granma to do
but survey children wall to wall
and beam with joy
on that magic, blissful evening,
when life was as it should be—

not knowing that soon her son would die.

THE DADDY SOUND

I heard the "Daddy Sound,"
    the reassuring, comfort sound
he, and only he, could make
    to which I often fell asleep.

It was an evening sound,
    an after-bedtime sound,
which sometimes I could hear,
    and knew I was protected.

It was his sound, and his alone;
    softly, rhythmic, and yet a roughness.
It was a magic part of childhood,
    a magic moment I could hear.

I grew up, moved away and married,
    began a family of my own,
and forgot the special
    Daddy Sound

Then one ordinary day,
    after relaxing shower,
I calmly thoughtfully scratched myself
    and heard a buried memory:

The "Daddy Sound" from long ago.
    Stunned in shock, I stood
and realized what I'd been hearing
    and treasured in those years.

That special, magic sound, so comforting,
    was mundane, simple—and somewhat crude.
My father was simply, leisurely—
    scratching his hairy behind.

LITTLE SISTER LOST

The little boy and girl
    had gone to play
        in grass as tall as they,
valiantly
    they pushed down grass
        to make halls and rooms:
living room, kitchen,
    bedrooms, too;
        with halls between.
Dinner was eaten
    and babies
        put down to nap,
suddenly
    little sister was gone:
        vanished!
The boy panicked:
    where could she be?
        Just disappeared!!
Momma was calm,
    unworried,
        they began to search.
Calling her name
    woke her up
        rubbing sleep
from her eyes
    where she had napped
        with her baby doll.

PIGS IN A BLANKET

Not a blanket, actually,
    but a towel, or several.
We wrapped the pigs in them
    to conserve their warmth.
They were tiny, born too early,
    and could easily die.
The mother, with her bulk,
    four—five hundred pounds,
could easily crush them
    and not even notice:
they were so tiny,
    she was so huge.
And the barn was cold, so cold,
    and freezing wind blew through,
they could not live there
    and would surely die,
so we wrapped them snug
    and put them on the open oven door.

TIRED MAN

Tired.
    He was so tired:
        always tired.

He worked eighteen-hour days
    in summer,
        fifteen in winter.

No one ever said, "Thank you,"
    or even knew
        what to be thankful for.

He was removed
    before we were aware
        of all we needed of him.

The picture shows a different man,
    a happy man:
        one smiling.

I do not remember
    nor recognize—
        his smile.

His last day was in the field,
    working still.
        He worked himself to death.

The tractor drove
    across his body
        crushing bone and tissue.

He was a tired man,
    at least now—
        he has his rest.

THE MORNING DADDY DIED

The dream came true
　　the morning daddy died:
the rainbow in the dream
　　led to pegasus in colors,
beautiful rainbow colors
　　entrance a little girl.
Pegasus became a car
　　flying in the sky
and in the car was Daddy
　　flying high.
She wants to go with Daddy,
　　safe in his strong arms,
"You can't come with me now,"
　　said Daddy, waved goodbye.
Alone, the little girl
　　did not understand,
until, ten years later—
　　the morning Daddy died.

CONNECTIONS

Decisions of one generation
    change the course of lives
and sets the future different
    than it might have been.
By such decisions
    we are all connected,
entwined through centuries,
    decisions cascading over lives;
generation to generation
    without end.
We can never know
    what impact will result
of a decision now,
    this is our turn.
The mystery of connection
    links us all together
as our lives
    weave their way through time.

HOME TO BAYERN

My grandfather
    never missed
        the hills of Franken,
He never walked the streets
    of Reckendorf,
        his family "hometown."
He would have been amazed
    to see the things
        his father took for granted.
He did not learn,
    "Gruess Gott,"
        as the common greeting,
Nor did he plow
    the family fields
        of Bayern.
He lived
    a continent away
        and never knew his family.
A grandson went,
    a century after,
        to find the home and people;
His heart leapt
    and wept for joy
        in reunion.
Deutscher und Amerikaner:
    alles ein Famalia—
        It's been so long...

DESTINY

The father bid farewell
    knowing he would never see
        his namesake son again

And died of a broken heart.

To save him
    he had to send him
        to a foreign land
        forever.

If not,
    the new Kaiser's army
        would take him
        and destroy him.

Each would never see the other again.

In the foreign land,
    far, far away,
        the boy and family grew;

Thriving, generations later,
    because of the pain
    and sacrifice
        of one father and son.

Back at home
    the family died
        due to one war or another.

I cannot give sufficient thanks
    to Andreas (the elder),
    and Andreas, his son:
        Urgrossvater Meine.

FAMILY MAN

Sitting on the front porch
    proud:
Andreas und Frau
    und Kind—Carl,
on a homestead claim
    in Amerika land:

Ein mann,
    mit Haus, und Frau und Sohn.

Behind the family group,
    a blanket made
with skills from "the old country"
    where a man could not
make himself anew
    if need be.

Here was success
    "American Style,"
and proud of it
    in 1898!

IN FRANKEN

The little shrine by the way
    with a history no one knows—
"It's been there forever,"
    like the mountains.
The land is dotted
    with these little shrines,
markers of devotion
    and symbols of the faith.
They add a richness to the land,
    a reminder to us now:
this land you see
    is more than dirt and trees,
it holds the souls
    past more than we can know;
people lived and died and prayed
    as some day you will too:
continue on your way—
    beyond this mortal life.

MOTHER TONGUE

The grown man,
   with no recollection
      of the foreign words,
Is, nonetheless, stirred
   deep, deep within,
      in his sacred place.
The sounds and syllables
   comfort him
      and caress his soul.
Where does this comfort, assurance,
   and familiarity,
      come?
The man is mystified—
   where is the connection?
      The sounds are so true.
Yet, no one speaks these words.
   Finally he remembers
      the great grandfather.
Though he died long ago,
   when the man was little,
      not yet five,
the first of his generation
   and, being male,
      would carry the name.
He was special to the old man
   who had left his home and family
      to save the name.
"Where's my boy!"
   he would demand.
      The boy would run and love him.

The boy tamed him
    for he was tough;
        immigrant on his own,
he made his way, and succeeded
    far from all he knew
        and loved.

He did not tame easily,
    stubborn as the mules he drove
        and cussed in German,
causing sounds to ring
    across the Kansas fields
        (his temper was renowned).
He cussed his son
    and others,
        and drove the next away,
But he did not cuss this boy,
    with this boy he was tender,
        age too, had softened him.
He would speak softly to the boy,
    and what better words
        than his mother tongue?

Spreichts du Deutsch, mein enkelkind?
    Ich gelehrsamkeit,
        Urgrossvater, meine.

ROLLING SEAS

I do not live near the ocean
    and never slept by its roar.

I live near a different sea
    whose waves whisper under wind.
Green makes a softly brushing sound,
    then golden scratching rustle.

How alike the two seas are
    under the blazing sun,
clouds causing each
    to grow in different ways.

One with life below,
    mine with life in view:
from tiny sprouts
    to final harvest.

A sea of green turning gold,
    changing with the seasons;
rolling seas of wheat
    surround my prairie home.

NIGHT VISITS

The little child slept
   his troubled sleep
when panic woke him in the dark
    feeling little feet
    (and brush of wings),
   sure the wasps would sting.

Too terrified to scream
    or move, or even breathe,
   the midnight seconds passed.

Bedroom windows had no screens
    and wasps would fly inside
   looking for a home.

Sometimes they found his face
    or dropt
   little balls of mud.

Little feet were crawling
    on him;
   tiny little feet:
    on his face,
     across his cheek.

TRAVELING

Going out to the woods
    with a book,
  sitting on a hill
    with trees for company:
  there is no greater bliss.

The wind moves gently
    across the page,
  birds proclaim their joy
    and shade dabbles
  space around my feet.

I am alone in time
    and eternity,
  with a book I step
    out of my life and place,
  into some where else.

CAUGHT IN THE AIR

Suspended,
    as if on a string,
struggling,
    fluttering,
trying with all it's might
    to fly.
All the energy the bird
    expends
is only enough
    to keep it
suspended,
    in the same place.
It struggles
    then turns
and dives away
    to freedom,
no longer prisoner
    of the wind.

DYSLEXIC

I remember reading,
   the funny shapes and squiggles
were supposed to correspond
   with nonsense sounds.

My teacher kindly
   kept trying, trying and trying.
By the end of summer—
   I could really read.

At least I don't remember
   not-reading after then,
but the words still flopped on pages
   and letters do trade places.

But I fought to control them
   and still do.
To win, I've learned some tricks,
   and learned them well.

Other teachers said,
   "…not using his potential."
Oh, how little they knew
   the struggle to hold them straight.

Not only now I read,
   but write too. Words:
thousands, millions of words
   and most of them are straight.

But I remember backwards
   and the kindness of Miss Warner
who, patient, taught me
   the code and sound of squiggles.

COMMUNING

The pine trees,
The circle of pines,
In the yard:
    the circle of pines.
The boy was loosing his mind.

The walls of school were blurred
    and closing in around him.
The halls changed colors,
    as he concentrated on his way.
The days merged together…
    he could not remember…

The pines
    in a circle
    whispered to the boy…
        And he joined them.

Lying in their midst,
    surrounded by those friends
he felt assured that something
    would remain secure and stable.
The pines…knew his pain
    and whispered him asleep.

When he awoke
    it was not so hard to tie his shoes
And he could again decide
    what to eat.

As he walked
he saw
    things once more that were the same.
He was glad,
    and did not suffer so.

To welcome him back home
The pines
    waved their needles, whispered
    and sang a lullaby.
He closed his eyes
    in gratitude…
    and slept.

THE GREATEST GIFT

For the son who wanted to write
   the gift was a sign
     of approval,
the first indication
   of acceptance
     of the dream.
He knew that typing was the key,
   so practiced
     assiduously.
The gift was her own,
   almost antique,
     Remington portable
given to her by her father,
   for college
     and a new life.
The son also was going
   to college
     where he typed and typed:
on his knees, in the car,
   on his desk,
     anywhere needed.
He typed with joy and sang:
   "This
     is who I was meant to be."
His words found homes
   in places
     of the globe far away.
They enriched the lives
   of untold numbers—
     for this is who he was meant to be.

TIME WHEN

My face is pressed against the glass
    by a force I cannot stop.
I saw the glass wall coming,
    but could not stop it either.

There is life on the other side
    but I can not yet go through,
The glasswall barrier
    marks a time in my life.

I am my father's oldest age
    and soon:
        it will be time for us to die.

TIME: ONE

The flower blooms at forty-two;
    forty-two petals with forty-two lives.

Streaking from the caverns of despair
    the flame shoots to the stars.

Limits are broken and darkness is gone:
    yesterday was so far away.

Colors burst from nuggets hidden
    for protection deep within.

The flower nods in the breeze
    and stretches out for rain.

THE BOX

The box needs to be a box
  because it only knows
    it is a box.
It knows
  because it has been told:
    THIS IS A BOX.
But,
  would it be a box
    if it knew
One's identity
  is determined
    by one's thoughts and actions?
The Box
  can be anything
    it wishes to be
If only it dared
  to think
    outside the box.
Though most limits
  are imposed,
    created by others
And adopted
  or assumed
    without thought:
We can be ANYTHING
  we decide and strive
    to be.

MOVING WATER

There is something about water,
    moving water,
even if the water
    is not all moving,
just ripples across the top—
    it is the motion.
This water answers
    something deep
within ourselves
    we don't even know
yet come back
    again and again and again.
Does the water in us
    (sixty-eight percent)
recognize
    the vast and greater water
we can see,
    and know that it is life?

FLIGHT

A flock of eye-glasses swimming
     in the clouds
    with wings of brilliant hue
Pass by
    leaving the mind amazed.

Where does the journey go?
     and when?

Sapphire seas rustle on the shore
    calling: "Come! Come!"

My knees are frozen
     and feet fixed in sand,
    no motion but wish.

Turning inward, in, in:
    the real true journey,

Without which
    we die.

So we try, and we try,
    and try.

HE WAITED

The elderly man
    was sitting in the house
waiting for his wife
    to arrive.

He knew she would return,
    this was their home
exactly as they left it
    years ago.

the view outside
    was also just
as he remembered:
    familiar, secure.

I saw him there,
    in my dream,
my grandfather,
    waiting after death.

I tried to tell him,
    "You can leave,
you don't have to sit
    here forever.

"Your possibilities
    are limitless—
go anywhere,
    do anything."

No, he would sit
    and wait for her:
Granma would know
    what to do.

She had not yet died
    so he waited
But did not mind:
    he KNEW she would come.

When her time came
    they went out together
to tend the flowers
    with new-found wings.

AUTUMN MESSENGERS

A smudge on the horizon
    becomes little, wavering lines,
These, in turn, become
    separate flying dots,
the dots, in turn become, geese
    honking on their way,
warning of winter freezing:
    "Make way, make way.
The frozen time is coming.
    Flee to warmth and life."
They signal the turn of a year
    the harvest must be gathered,
a year of growth has ended,
    prepare for winter's blast.
The geese have warned us,
    we have not much time
to prepare, for soon
    we must be snug inside.

FIRE IN THE SNOW

Gently falling snow
    melting in the heat,
yellow leaping flames
    pushing back the cold:
an amazing combination
    of opposites.
The gentle hiss of drops
    falling on the fire
compliments the creek nearby
    gurgling away.
Silent countryside is broken
    by one lonely crow
and a tiny flock of geese
    passing overhead;
two brothers tending wood
    to feed the fire,
cutting cedars
    to keep the pasture clean.

WINTER'S LAST STAND

This has become a day of ice;
    window screens opaqued.
Ice trees near are silver,
        silent,
            gripped with death;
Weeds and grasses frozen
        fragments
        of living yesterdays:
Winter's Last Stand.

A few days more: Náw-Ruz
        And Spring.
An icy day of winter to remind us
    of the past.
The new year is resistless,
    as is the Day of God.

WAITING FOR SPRING

The little pond
    in the meadow
covered half with ice
    is waiting
for the willow to bloom
    on its bank,
and the cat tails
    to burst their seeds,
and the frogs to crawl
    from their safe place
and sing the joy
    of Spring!
That day will come
    when hearts will melt
and faith will shine
    from every face
and Spring will glow
    in every heart.

CHICKEN CREEK ROAD

No up-scale suburb, this!
"Chicken Creek Road"
named because of—what?

Obviously:
chickens were in the creek.
At least,
at some memorable moment.

The possibilities are wild:
chickens everywhere!
up and down the creek!
chickens in the trees and the bushes!

This is:
local color,
a homespun name,
not easily ignored.

Who can ever forget
an address on:
Chicken Creek Road?

HAYS BOOT HILL

They died with their boots on
   so the legend goes,
      and maybe some of them did.
Others just died
   by disease or stupidity,
      or accidents of life.
They no longer lie here;
   a decision was made
      to move them away.
Now houses stand
   and streets cut through
      the once-burying ground.
When it rained,
   my landlord said,
      her sons would find little bones:
Finger bones or toe bones,
   they could not find them all
      when the graves were moved.
Now a marker says
   "Boot Hill"
      and a bench is placed to sit,
But it's more a tourist site;
   no cemetery,
      no memories remain.
The "real" Boot Hill
   is in our minds
      and legends.

COLORADO LOOMS

Driving the high plains of western Kansas,
    Colorado looms
unseen over the far horizon,
    but not unfelt.

Highway signs proclaim: "so many miles
    to Colorado."
(it is the only place
    worth going to.)

People of the steppes of Kansas—windblown,
    are far from the lights
of Kansas City, St. Louis,
    or Chicago.

In the invisible, but pervasive shadow,
    of the Rocky Mountains,
felt far in the west,
    they work and die.

They are not part of Colorado,
    and the mineral history
of Denver…
    is not their own.

These patient, tried, enduring farmers,
    and workers of the plains,
the true heart of Kansas,
    are lost among
the wind and open spaces; over which unseen,
    Colorado looms.

Wind and open spaces—calling:
    Colorado.

DAILY RUN

They race:

four inches at a time;
    wavering frail arms
place the walker ahead
    with great deliberation.

"Beat'cha this time, Ethel!"
    calls the winner
with a gleam in her wrinkled eyes
    reaching the dinning room door.

"There's always tomorrow."
    retorts the other
only inches behind,
    losing just for the day.

THE PLASTIC SNAKE IS DEAD

Placed on boards in the rafters
    the plastic snake
was a warning to the birds:
    "Do not nest here
this place is not safe, see—
    here is a snake!"
One bird believed too well
    and attacked.
The snake did not fare well,
    torn in half
and pecked to pieces,
    it ended on the ground.
Such ferocity and courage
    amazed the humans
who did not attempt to tamper
    with instincts of the brave.
A different solution
    will be tried next year.

LONELY UNIVERSE

Pictures of other planets;
　　show moons, rings and rocks…
　　　　(it's lonely there)

Seeing crater-marked globes, barren,
　　unearthly beauty, but…
　　　　(no life or love).

The space between is vast,
　　our efforts tiny, frail;
　　　　the task to learn so great.

More precious now, our life on earth,
　　(varied, diverse and plentiful)
　　　　we cannot waste.

Were this one lost
　　(whatever reason)
　　　　there is no other.

Precious, precious;
　　all life
　　　　is our trust.

SOCIAL MORTIFICATION

Aunt was crying,
    the children were distressed:
        adults did not often cry;
Some disaster
    must have occurred
        to cause such distress.
A family party
    was in progress
        to celebrate a grand event,
so grand—there was a crowd
    all their friends
        had come:
all the important people,
    socially correct
        and Victorianly polite.
On this day,
    of all days,
        the grandmother, upstairs,
With a mind of her own
    and
        more wayward than a child,
threw,
    from her chamber window,
        onto the roof below
For all to see—
    the contents
        of her chamber pot!

"TO MAKE THE WORLD SAFE..."

Rotting corpses flung
    from shallow graves
wearing uniforms and medals
    new a month ago
as the ground is plowed
    by this week's bombs.

"Over the top, Boys!"
    the commander sings
and dies.

We will all die.
    We are all dead.
This war
    will kill us all.

"To make the world safe
    for Democracy..."
will make the world safe
    for no one.

Not even the dead
    can rest today.

AFRICAN DIGNITY

News photos
    are world-wide witness
    of her respect:

Little shoes carefully
    side by side
    on a tree stump.

They were new;
    her father
    had just bought them,

"For my princess,"
    with a smile
    as wide as love.

When macheties came
    she knew,
    and placed them carefully

to protect them
    for the next
    little girl.

INTO MORNING

The globe turns
  slowly (so slow)
  into the light,
  almost
  as if it did not at all.

Branches line
  against the sky
  new patterns
  form
  so faintly to be seen.

People too,
  turn slowly,
  one by one
  into the light:
  we wonder if they turn at all.

Nations ponder
  and vacillate,
  agonize
  and politic
  yet movement creeps along.

Turn they do
  into the light
  and soon the night
  will pass at last
  for darkness has no power.

Turning from
  the darkness,
  ignorance and fear
  will clutch no longer
  hearts and minds of humankind.

DAWN LIGHT

Gently waking the world;
    dawn light.
Time for early chores—
    animals stir.

Farm boy pausing at the gate,
     chants with rising sun:
    Alláh'u'Abhá,
    Alláh'u'Abhá,
    Alláh'u'Abhá.

Another day's begun.

    God is All Glorious,
    He is All Glorious,
     Verily:
    The All Glorious.

SEEING

The bell rings
    deeply, resonating
    rising high
    into the sky

The earth recedes—
    tiny seeds
    of consciousness
    grow:

This world's our own,
    one home,
    our only home;

One,
    for all mankind,
    one humankind:
    one people…
Home…
one planet…

NOW.

QUIET AND PEACE

Be still.
    Silent
    as a solitary cloud
    in the sky,
    or moon
    full of light.

Be still.
    Silent,
    let it rest:
    your mind
    and your body;
    let it rest.

Be still.
    Silent,
    from the depths
    of the well
    of peace:
    let silence flow.

Be still.
    Silent,
    as the stars
    in their courses
    circling round
    the planet.

Be still.
    Silent,
    breathe
    slowly, softly,
    with meaning

Be still.
    Silent,
    rest,
    as the rocks repose
    in their might
    and strength.

Be still.
    Silent,
    as the flower opens
    softly to the sun,
    and glorifies
    it's Lord.

Be still.
    Silent,
    open to the Spirit
    whispering
    softly
    in your heart.

Be still.
    Silent
    in the rhythm and flow
    of the soul
    of the world.
    with meaning and grace.

BUFFALO SPIRIT

Giant beasts of the plains
    across the hillside
calmly eating their way
    in one direction.

Calves are mixed in the herd
    with their mothers
who all have horns
    and the humps of their age.

Once great multitudes roamed
    these endless seas
of grass and sky,
    great thundering herds.

Now the herds are fenced
    and restricted
to places here and there,
    they cannot roam at will.

Still, they remain
    awesome beasts:
awesome and amazing,
    huge and fearsome..

Once indispensable
    to prairie life,
they are now curiosities,
    a reminder of the past.

They allow our imagination
	to join them in another time,
to become with them
	free spirits and roam

Over hills and valleys
	of spiritual adventure,
to thunder unrestrained
	over prairies of possibilities.

Buffalo are now a symbol
	of our souls,
to be and grow
	as God intended.

WEDDING DANCE

A wedding
    on a hill
    on the rolling prairie
    on the first day of the year;

A new year
    and new life
    together.

Rising sun
    and gentle rain
    will bless our way
as we face this union
    of hearts
    and minds
    and souls.

With friends we gather
    to celebrate life,
    new life,
    and great love.

We greet this day
    and year
    and life
    with hearts full
        and brimming—

Love floweth over
    and joy,
    and joy,
    and joy…

LIGHTLY TREADING

To be respectful of The Mother
 we must step lightly
  when walking on her.

Our treading must not be
 a cause of sorrow or disruption;
  for others must pass too.

Behind us we must leave
 a trail of Beauty—
  in faces, places and planets;

A Trail of Beauty to resound
 in Glory dancing on the waves
  of human tracing.

LIGHTENING IN THE SKY

Brilliant flashes
    each unique
        herald the coming storm.
The midnight light
    illuminates
        hidden, secret crimes.
Eighteen flashes lit the night
    waking souls,
        to herald the Day of God.
From Mulla Husayn,
    the first to find
        The Point,
To Quddus,
    the last and
        Hidden Treasure,
And the Poetess,
    Solace of the Eyes,
        The Trumpet Blast.
Each lightening flash
    exposed
        a crumbling way,
Their example redefined
    a life of sacrifice,
        and they remain
Dawnbreakers,
    awakeners
        of a new Day.

IN THE DIM LIGHT

In the dim light we stand
  seeing no end
    but promise.
In the dim light we try
  to reach but find
    empty air.
In the dim we see imperfectly
  the way and means
    of love.
Dim down to nothing
  we sometimes fall
    but not all.
In the dim day faintly we
  can almost see
    a reason.
In the dim we try heroically
  to rise above
    the mire.
The dim light does not stop us
  but propels
    our hope.

Some days, hours or moments
  we succeed,
    if not...
It is our earnestness
  that saves
    us all.

TRYING TIMES

This darksome land,
this feeble age
    with dim, uncomprehending minds
      worshiping ruins
        and
      truth distorted:

The few
    keep trying, trying, trying…
    and try again.

Some labor brings forth fruit
    that can been seen
      as evidence,
    others only hope.

Stumbling in the dark
    we fall and trip
    ourselves and others.

There are no stairs.

The light is dimly reaching
    at times
    or flooding in a heart,
      inarticulate
      but sincere.

With courage
    we carry on
    in trying times.

POETS CRY

All the poets cry aloud,
    the earth is in its weeping.
Among the silent, deaf and dumb
    the Poet-Singer knows
The earth in its travail
    begetting a new vision.
Mankind suffers agony
    as hearts sicken groan and die.
Traditions creak and crumble,
    their age cannot sustain…
Now the Scattering Angels
    work their mercy-vengeance.
See the order in the chaos?
    As the poets cry aloud.
New forms, ideas, ways
    slowly are constructed
realizing a new vision,
    and poets cry aloud.

IN THE DARKNESS SHINES

What manner of light,
in the darkness shines
unearthly and unreal?

Transcendent
and awe-spiring,
it glances on our lives.

In the darkness surely,
when the soul is tried.
We see the light most real.

This LIGHT,
illumination,
shows the way to grow.

In the darkness shines
the Light Divine
into the depths of pain.

For if we see,
we will transcend
the limits of our selves.

"And they have made their dwelling,
in the shadow of the Essence."

GENESIS II

Neutrons explode!
Electrons dance in ecstasy
and dissolve!
Protons expire in bliss.
Quarks, nutrinos,
leptons and haptons
dance their death.

Omnipotence unleashed:
Genesis again,
through the power of the word:
"BE!"
and It Is Done.

All of creation
is re-created in an instant.

THIS is Ridván!!
The Paradise and Divine Springtime.

Mere mortals move
if they perceive
the blinding knowledge:
Omnipotent NOW,
invoking new beings
to sustain the Mighty Word
unleashed
to ravage the universe:
destroy and rebuild
on a new foundation.

New laws of spiritual power
set in operation
to transform
the very molecules,
every created thing
and new human beings.

This is the new creation,
Ridván: The Dawn
of the maturity
of the human race.

SOUL MONARCH

The King of Glory
   reigns
      through chaos, confusion
         and transformation.

Weak lives—
Broken hearts—
Shattered cultures—
      are all transmuted
      into new creations.

Inward real
    to the heart
        changes penetrate;
Rearranging molecules
    and atoms of the soul.

There is no end
    to maelstrom matrix:
        beyond our power,
        or comprehension.

Fortunate are they
    who fling themselves
    into the Sun:
"Gold! Here I come—
      through the fiery furnace…"
    copper is transmuted.

Alchemy
   of souls
      complete.

SUN MAGNIFICENT

Bahá'u'lláh:
the Sun Magnificent,
has rearranged the soul
and body and heart
of generations.

Dynamic destinies await
those millions who
fling themselves into the Sun—
becoming stars.

Hesitation kills
the soul in some degrees
Run! Leap! Jump!
Into life with God!

Bahá'u'lláh fulfills
the ancient need
and mystic union
with absolute reality
and sacredness.

Exaltation rings
from one so unattached;
transcendent,
leaving self
and nothingness.

Bahá'u'lláh, the Sun
consumes, renews, transforms
the dust
into Magnificence!

IN WONDER

Surging from the sky
singing praises
to the One
Who originated
all being,
came they.
Multitudes of praise
pour forth,
range upon range
in ecstasy.
Colors
transcending the rainbow
in waves
vibrantly dancing on air.

This is the living,
This is the joy,
This is the purpose
beyond breath.

SURRENDER

The crystal air behind the "real"
    is truth in fact.

The oneness of all things—
    flowing power overwhelms

A little mind at prayer
    loosing hold of one "reality."

Seeing peace beyond the war
    and fellowship transcendent.

Prayer inarticulate,
    is replaced by muffled sobs.

Some say: "crazy," others nod
    with wisdom of their years.

To pray, to give—surrender human will
    to the one Benevolent One:

There is no other purpose, life,
    or direction for existence.

Exhaustion, exaltation and collapse.
    So be it.

TIMES, NOW

Time doesn't answer,
    it passes by
        slowly or lurching
we never know.
People, bewildered,
    longing for assurance:
        life was good once,
    but they forget,
Forget the uncertainties
    that were survived
        by others
        not affecting them,
And uncertainties now
    will pass in time
        forgotten;
    only our progress
Will be noted and envied:
    that so much could be done
        by so few
    and so tried.
It is not who we are
    but what we do
        despite
    the uncertainties now.
Change is painful
    but necessary
        for the *now* to be bettered
    for future,

Because our striving
       is our salvation
             and the world's,
       and victory
Will come
       on the wings
             of exhaustion
       and hope.

TRANSFORMATION

The Point of Utter Helplessness
    is a bewilderment
    or nonsense,
    to those of yet
    not reached it.
To the one who has arrived,
    that Point
    is a line divide:
    life before,
    and nothing after.
That Point erases
    one's self;
    all
    that you thought you were:
    is gone.
The Void of Helplessness
    swallows you,
    consumes
    all that you knew
    you were.
Questions come:
    What to do?
    Where to turn?
    What to learn?
    Who am I now?
Eventually
    a part of life
    can be rebuilt
    over wreckage
    and debris.

It is a different life
because you are
a different soul,
who has been tested
and transformed:
Now a new creation.

GOLDEN ALCHEMY

Crucibles of pain
transmute
the clay
into purest gold.

The fire cries:
"Change, change;
Melt away imperfection,
Vaporize the mist.
Luster gleaming
shall
be thy reward."

Searing soul experience:
"I'm dying…
I'm dying…
I'm…

Gone.

The pieces don't remain,
They now BE
something new:

Newly created ones
who speak
new words,
new forms,
new vision.

A new song
fills new hearts
with new worlds.

SOUL JOURNEY

The journey of the soul
   unwinds, rewinds,
expands, compresses
   and continues to change.

The growing soul alters
   perception and direction
seeking the open way
   despite difficulties and trials.

The adventurer knows
   behind whirlwind lies calm,
past chaos is peace,
   beyond torment is grace.

The traveler sees above
   apparent limits,
the valleys of illusions
   to the mountain of certitude.

Within the heart, tenderly,
   the seeker carries hope
and listens to the quiet whispers:
   "peace."

Temptations abound
   to give up, relax and forget,
but Truth
   is a higher goal.

Distractions continually assail
   the earnest one,
but stamina is exercised
   and prevails.

Eventually…
   the height of attainment
is achieved
   and the vista is clear.

Up ahead, through the mist,
   another goal is perceived.
For growth
   never ends…

STRUGGLE TO THE DISTANT SHORE

The passions of life surge around us
    pulling one way,
    urging another,
    pleading…
Yet, we can not follow
    for the depths are great
    and we are not strong.
To swim against the current
    is tiring,
    but it is the only way
        to reach the shore.
Millions pass by (and die)
    on their way of ease
    and ignorance,
But we aim higher,
    above the norm,
    for there is firm footing
        and reunion.

It is Reunion that pulls us on:

Reunion
    with joy and love and exaltation,
Reunion
    with all that is most wonderful,
Reunion
    that will embrace and lift the soul,
Reunion
    that will banish all pain,
Reunion;
    when I can finally rest.

In that hope
     I carry on,
Struggle
     and strive to attain,

The Distant Shore.

THE ACHING CONTROL OF DESIRE

The feel of arms and lips and fingers
    on your body
    on my body
        cannot be realized.

A higher purpose awaits
    in place of fleeting gratification.

The pain of renunciation
    wrings my soul,
        yet this is best:

To do without in one little life
    for the greater life that is to come.

The aching control of desire now
    will release stupendous passion
    later
    when it can be returned
        in full measure.

GARDEN OF THE ROSE

The Garden of the Rose
   summons wretched flowers
      from the desert
for transformation:
   liberation, resurrection,
      and the chance to be a rose.
The Garden of the Rose
   is open to all people.
      Some pass by unseeing.
Some wander in then out.
   Some stop to destroy
      (they cannot live with Beauty).
The Garden of the Rose
   is dwelt within by lovers—
      lovers who cannot stay away;
lovers whose breath is life
   whose hearts are shining stars
      whose souls are soaring birds.
The Garden of the Rose
   endures supreme
      with ancient Beauty.
Renewed from age to age
   to rescue all lost flowers
      and welcome each one home,
In the Garden of the Rose
   where humankind
      can live in peace and joy.

SUPPLICATION

O My God.

O My Lord.

O My Master!

I beg Thee to forgive me
    for seeking:
any pleasure
    save Thy love,
any comfort
    except Thy nearness,
any delight
    besides Thy good pleasure,
any existence
    other than communion with Thee.

STEADFASTNESS

Toward the building of a world
that no one knows
and cannot see,
not even you or me.

A world beyond our farthest dreams—
but dreams can clash
and so can we.

A world beyond description—
but still our goal and aim;
we falter on—

one step at a time
we stumble and spill
yet continue,
against all odds—

Toward the building of a world
that no one knows
and cannot see,
not even you, or me.

SAY, "PEACE."

They say, "Peace,"
    with a club.
They say, "Peace,"
    with a sword.
They say, "Peace,"
    with a gun.
They say, "Peace,"
    with a bomb.
They say, "Peace,"
    with a missile.

And-there-is-no peace-at-all;

When, "Peace," is called
    with a pen,
      will they listen?

"O Rulers of the earth!
    Be reconciled among your selves…"
"O Representatives of the people,
    Take ye council together…"

Thus sayeth unto you,
    the Pen of the Most High.

"These fruitless strifes,
    these ruinous wars
      shall pass away,
      and the Most Great Peace
        shall come."

GOD TOOK A CHANCE

God took a Hugh Emery Chance
   and made of him
   a builder of the Kingdom.

He was not the first Hugh Emery Chance
   but he was the first Chance
   God took for Himself.

God took this Chance
   to Israel, the Holy Land,
   to build God's Holy Mountain.

This was the Chance
   to begin the House of Justice
   that "source" free from error.

This Chance spread well
   the laws of God
   round the planet round.

This Chance of God
   built up the Seat
   of the Law of God.

And it was this Chance too
   to terrace the mount
   and complete the Arc.

This Chance of God
   earned well his rest,
   God will not need another.

EAGLE IN A SARI

The eagle in the sari,
    roaring from the mountain top,
appears so insignificant
    and frail.
But the Voice of God,
    has hold of her and calls
across the continents:
    "This is no mortal here,
But the Greatest Name of God."
    She will emphasize and tell of
the Creator, specks of dust
    and future blazing suns.
Her teacher: Saint Martha Root,
    Commander: The Sign of God,
Director, the House, source of all good
    and free from error.
Mehrangiz Munsiff,
    is not so insignificant or frail.

ANGELS IN SEPARATION

Angels weep in separation,
    distant
from the Court of Glory.

The fire of their love
    would consume them
but for their tears.

Chained in bodies
    in the world of names,
afflictions abound.

They yearn for peace,
    reunion and release
from self.

Patience, patience:
    pain is fleeting,
patience.

Time will come
    when time
will be no more.

The journey,
    long,
will end in bliss and union.

Peae and joy
    will be the prize
for faithfulness,

In Glory, upon Glory
    and, forevermore:
LIGHT!.

POEM OF DEDICATION

A Center,
A place,
"Blessed is the spot, and the house, and the place…"

A century since the beginning
    here, in Wichita,
    the center of the nation.

This
    "remote and extensive country,"
now has a spot
blessed and dedicated
to the Most Great Name.

The second Bahá'í community
    (Kansas)
west of Egypt,

Now,
    one hundred and five years
since it's beginning
has born fruit:
    physical evidence
    of endurance
    and growth and progress.

From this Center
    will beam rays
    of prayer, hope and love

Showing a new way
    to reunion
    and the unity
    of all mankind.

This Center,
    this blessed spot,
    this focal point,
will serve to call
    to all of Kansas

In the Name
    of the Most Holy,
    the Most Great:
    Bahá'u'lláh.

STORY OF A LIFE

The weight.

The weight is tremendous
and he staggers.

He staggers
but
does not fall.

The weight paralyzes
him
sometimes
and he cannot move.

Other times
he carries it
and even,
once in a while,
does not notice.

But the weight takes its toll
even when he does not notice:
it colors
and informs
his view of the world.

Some of the weight
is permanent,
some of the weight
he pries off
in painful pieces,
some
he uses to build.

In two ways
he uses the weight:
this, I will not do.
I will resist,
no matter how painful;
other pain
he uses as blocks
to build his future.

These building blocks,
here, and there, and there,
are pieces of my life
now
transformed
into part of a new thing
with no relation
to what
it once was.

TAKING STRANGERS IN

Wayfarers passing by:
    the ill, the young
    the helpless,
Gathered from the highway
    on a cold wet day—
    strangers all,
Hearts offering shelter,
    fellowship,
    humanity.
Extraordinary acts of kindness
    in an untamed sea
    of materialism;
Awesome acts
    of the human sprit
    in an age of greed.
It is such acts
    that are sung for ages
    when times say, "No."
Apocalyptic epochs
    don't allow
    such kindness of heart,
Yet hearts are kind,
    loving, generous,
    despite the times,
Proof like no other
    of the enduring truth
    of spiritual beings.

NOBLE LIGHT

"I have made thee
    a being of Light,
wherefore
    (why?)
doest thou hide thyself
    in darkness."

We are Light
    it is our soul:
eternal, brilliant,
    everlasting.
Yet
    we try not to see,
and stay, therefore, blind
    to this Light
in ourselves
    and others:
Noble
    of Light

DUANAKA HASANUKA

Two brothers,
  separated by distance
  but not time or place.

Two who share,
  one love,
  for the Blessed Beauty.

Two who live
  to serve the world—
  their brothers and sisters.

Two languages in common:
  one of words,
  one of spirit.

Two who build
  new institutions
  of a new world.

Two histories:
  one lost,
  one found.

In union
  their histories merge
  into one adventure.

Living in two hearts:
  heart of Asia,
  heart of America,

But in one place:
  the realm
  of their Beloved.

"PERFECTION IS NOT…"

It was not the perfect party
    though you tried
    to be the perfect host.

The beverage mix
    was either watery
    or too thick.

The offered brownies
    carried bits of shell
    mixed in the nuts.

It was nearly a disaster;
    Jan and Jean were leaving
    and things weren't right.

The picture saved the party.
    The artist cried, "It's perfect!"
    You wanly smiled.

At least "something" was done right.

The matting had reduced the sky
    directing sight
    to the focal point.

The gate of Bahji stood
    stretched out in all its glory:
    simply perfect.

It was a perfect party
    remembered years and years
    from that unlikely night.

Thank you,
    my dear Roger,
    and sadly, "Good Bye."

THE SECRET OF LIVING

A fountain springs up
    from the soul,
the nourishing life
    cools the air
bringing life, comfort and hope
    to those around.
Alone, he or she stands
    giving without expectation,
giving without asking
    or thinking of return.
It is the miracle
    of selflessness
that one soul offers
    its essence—for others.
This is the secret,
    of a truly lived life:
When we so give
    that others may grow, love and flourish.

THE PRISON OF SELF

In many disguises
    the prison of self
binds our lives
    with limits:
"I want, I need, I can't,"
    are familiar refrains
from those unwilling
    to break free.

Limits give comfort,
    security,
there is no challenge,
    no struggle, no pain.

It is beyond our self
    that we are truly free,
free to grow and become
    more than we thought
we could possibly be:
    truly to be free.

THE SEA OF DEEDS

On the Sea of Deeds
  our lives sail slowly,
one difficulty at a time
  as we define
who we are
  by what we do.

"Let deeds, not words
  be thine adorning,"
for our deeds
  transform our souls.

They are the fruit
  of our lives
and evidence
  of faith.

Deeds transform us
  from who we are,
to the soul
  we can become.

HERE AND —

Children come
   and go,
older people
   leave
and life goes on
   despite
whatever you
   do
and all too soon
   it is time
for you
   to move on too
as your place
   is taken
by others
   who build
their own lives
   on yours.

ALL THE WORLD'S A...

She overcame the screaming
and condemnation
of incompetence
to go on stage,
indulge the secret wish,
where, she found,
she could become her ancestors
who had lived it all before.

Now
she was performing art
and demonstrating
that pain is not a limit
but a step
in transformation.

In this role
and that,
she gave voice
to the voiceless
and found her own.

SUCCESS

You should have children.
Why?
Because it's fun for the children.

The innocent reply
was music
to the father's ears
who had wished,
as a child,
to have never been a child.

He knew
he had succeeded
in transforming his pain
into a life
of love and joy
for his own child.

Testimony
of a pure
and open child.

WHAT MORE, NOW?

He could not read.
He could not write.
The words and letters
would not hold still.
He never learned to spell
(and computers were invented!),
but he did not stop.
One country after another
saw his words in print;
past a dozen,
In his native English
then German, French,
and Dutch too!
What more can this boy do?
Farm boy has been transformed:
what limits cannot be
              trsnscended?

NOTES

Many poems in this collection have nine lines or nine stanzas or multiples of nine. This is in reference to the significance of the number nine in the name of Bahá'u'lláh. In the abjad reckoning, where letters of the alphabet are assigned a numerical value, the name "Baha" (the root word for Bahá'u'lláh), has the value of nine. A poem structured with the number nine is an indirect allusion to Bahá'u'llah and, therefore, a prayer.

Dawn Light: "Allah'u'Abhá," a form of the title, Bahá'u'lláh, meanings are given in the poem.

Duanaka, Hasanuka: "aka" (pronounced: aw-ka) added to an Uzbek name to indicate older brother, "uka" (eu-ka) is a younger brother.

Eagle in a Sari: dedicated to Mrs. Meherangiz Munsiff during a visit she made to Louhelen Bahá'í School. For most of her life she undertook nearly continuous travel teaching around the globe under the direction of the Guardian of the Bahá'í Faith, then the House of Justice; one of those indomitable women who have blazed the Light of Bahá'u'lláh in country after country after country.

Family Plowing: The word "machineries" is a term used by the author's grandfather to refer to all farm equipment too large to carry by hand—any kind of machinery. If it could be carried by hand it was a tool.

God Took A Chance: Presented by the author to Hugh (founding member of the international Bahá'í council) and Margaret Chance during Thanksgiving 1994 at their home in Winfield, Kansas. They were delighted.

<u>Home to Bayern</u>: "Bayern" is the native name of the state of Bavaria, in Germany, once an independent country, where the author's great grandfather was born.

<u>In Franken</u>: "Franken" (Franconia in English) is the native name of a section of northwest "Bayern," where the author's family originated. It was independently ruled by the Catholic bishop until Napoleon annexed it to Bavaria in the early 1800s.

<u>Into Morning</u>: World Healing Day, December 31, 6:00am, Topeka time.

<u>Lightening in the Sky</u>: "Dawnbreakers" is the collective designation for the earliest believers who prepared the way for the Bahá'í Faith. The names of three are found in the poem.

<u>Poem of Dedication</u>: This poem was written when the dedication of the Wichita Bahá'í Center was anticipated to be in August, or September or.... sometime in 2002. So the math is correct for that year—and when centuries are involved a few months are not so important.

"Blessed is the spot..." is the beginning phrase of one of the most familiar prayers of Bahá'u'lláh.

"A century since the beginning/here, in Wichita..." The earliest evidence of the Bahá'í Faith in Wichita comes from 1902. Two letters dated that year were written to believers in Wichita from 'Abdu'l-Bahá, son of Bahá'u'lláh. One of the letters states that the recipient had been able to, "guide Souls who are attracted to the Beauty of God and are enkindled by the fire of His love at this moment." If these souls were in Wichita, then an early Bahá'í community would have been present there in 1902. The only information known about them a century later is the names of the two who received the letters.

Fred G. Hale was listed in the 1902 Wichita city directory as a "trav man," meaning a traveling salesman, not a permanent resident. By the time his letter arrived he had returned home to Jersey City, New Jersey. The Wichita city directory gives his address as 430 S Market, though the letter had been addressed to him at 1936 N Lawrence. Enclosed with his letter was a letter to Frank Dyer. Sending one letter inside another was common practice for the time and the reply was returned the same way. Hale tried to locate Dyer in order to send the letter on to him, but he had moved from Wichita and by 1905 had not been found. Dyer is mentioned in two Wichita city directories: in 1900, living at 19th &

Water, and in 1902, at 1851 N Lawrence. He was a bookkeeper and unmarried. No further information is known about the Wichita Baha'is of 1902.

"Remote and extensive country..." this is a quote from the letter of 'Abdu'l-Bahá to Fred Hale. From Haifa, Palestine, one hundred years ago, Wichita would have been far way indeed, on the vast plains of North America.

"Most Great Name" is a reference to the name, Bahá'u'lláh.

"Second Bahá'í community/(Kansas)..." Kansas, generally, and Enterprise, Kansas specifically, was the site of the second Bahá'í community in the western hemisphere in 1897. Before that date the only Bahá'ís known to be in North or South America were in Chicago. There were no Bahá'ís yet in Europe. From Enterprise, Kansas one of the believers, Rose Hilty, moved with her family to Topeka in 1906. The Topeka Bahá'í community has been continuous from that date. So the Kansas Bahá'í community has been continuous since 1897.

"Endurance" Many things do not endure long in Kansas. Many ideas have come to Kansas and disappeared. The Bahá'í Faith came to Kansas and did not disappear. Not only has it endured here for more than a century now, but in that time the Kansas Bahá'í community has grown and thrived. This is definitely a story of success. The Bahá'í Faith is now an established part of Kansas.

Supplication: Based on a prayer revealed by the Báb, Herald and Forerunner of Bahá'u'lláh. The Guardian of the Bahá'í Faith wrote to an individual believer that it was, "advisable that the believers should make use, in their meetings, of hymns composed by Bahá'ís themselves, and also of such hymns, poems and chants, as are based on the Holy Words." (*Bahá'í Meetings*)

Bahá'í—Since 1969 Herrmann has been a member of the Bahá'í Faith after having been raised in a Lutheran (Missouri Synod) family. Some basic Bahá'í beliefs include affirming that the Bible is the Word of God, that Jesus is the virgin-born Son of God, that Jesus sacrificed Himself for the redemption of humanity, that Jesus ascended to the presence of God. And that good deeds, though essential, are secondary to faith. The second coming of Christ is a fact as well as the Christ Reality being the living manifestation of God. Bahá'ís are born again into the spirit of the Universal Christ which appears from age to age.

To be a Bahá'í one most accept Jesus Christ as the Son of God. This has been done by millions of Bahá'ís who were formerly Jews, Buddhists, Hindus, Zoroastrians, Muslims and others of no specific faith. The problem for others is the name. The name Bahá'í may be unfamiliar.

In the Book of Revelations are found several references to "a new name." Two of the verses clearly state: "(I) will give to him a white stone, and in the stone a new name." (2:17), and "I will write upon him my new name." (3:12). If the Book of Revelation is indeed, as Bahá'ís believe, "The Revelation of Jesus Christ, which God gave unto him, to shew unto his servants things which must shortly come to pass; and he sent and signified it by his angel unto his servant John," then it is Christ saying that there will be a new name by which to identify Him at a later time and will be identified with the revelation of God. Bahá'ís believe this new name is Bahá'u'lláh, the Prophet-Founder of the Bahá'í Faith.

Bahá'u'lláh means "Glory of God." There are many references in the Bible to the Glory of God coming and interacting in human affairs. Baha'is believe this is the age when those statements have become literally true.

In addition to affirming and promoting the person and station of Jesus Christ, other basic teachings of the Bahá'í Faith are that there is one Creator of the universe, though people call the Creator by different names, and the Creator has revealed His/Its will to the human race at different places and different times to enable the human race to advance as a species, and that the human race is in reality one race and we are each responsible for all of us and all life on earth.

In addition, each person has an eternal soul and the purpose of our life on earth is to develop our spiritual qualities so that when we leave this life we will be spiritually developed souls. The level of our spiritual development is demonstrated by the attributes we exhibit in this life, so we are to engage in society and help other individuals which also helps us grow.

The human race is, at the beginning of the 21st century, poised on the edge of a collective change. This change has been in progress for over a century and a half already and is an essential part of mankind's future. The change is a new orientation from a world of boundaries limiting individuals, their actions and point of view from what is tribal, racial, or national, etc. to embrace the whole planet and all of mankind. This is a gradual and inevitable transition, yet the change is not easy. It is and will be accompanied by chaos and fear because the unknown and new are always feared. Bahá'ís believe this change is part of the Will of God for this age and that God is ultimately in control.

Of particular interest to this farm boy poet is the level of importance given in Bahá'í scripture to the role of agriculture in the life of society. Agricultural is clearly regarded as the most important profession. So he looks forward to the day when farmers will be given the status and honor they deserve as being essential to the life of society.

Index of first lines

978-0-595-35051-3
0-595-35051-8